THIS IS ME! 2022

FEELS LIKE HOME

Edited By Sarah Waterhouse

First published in Great Britain in 2022 by:

Young Writers
Remus House
Coltsfoot Drive
Peterborough
PE2 9BF
Telephone: 01733 890066
Website: www.youngwriters.co.uk

Book Design by Ashley Janson

Softback ISBN 978-1-80015-998-3

Printed and bound in the UK by BookPrintingUK
Website: www.bookprintinguk.com
YB0505V

FOREWORD

For Young Writers' latest competition This Is Me, we asked primary school pupils to look inside themselves, to think about what makes them unique, and then write a poem about it! They rose to the challenge magnificently and the result is this fantastic collection of poems in a variety of poetic styles.

Here at Young Writers our aim is to encourage creativity in children and to inspire a love of the written word, so it's great to get such an amazing response, with some absolutely fantastic poems. It's important for children to focus on and celebrate themselves and this competition allowed them to write freely and honestly, celebrating what makes them great, expressing their hopes and fears, or simply writing about their favourite things. This Is Me gave them the power of words. The result is a collection of inspirational and moving poems that also showcase their creativity and writing ability.

I'd like to congratulate all the young poets in this anthology, I hope this inspires them to continue with their creative writing.

CONTENTS

Sacred Heart RC Primary School, Battersea

Western Primary School, Grimsby

THE POEMS

Me And My Best Friend

T ommy had a best friend called Gilbert.
O ff we went on an adventure.
M ove, Gilbert, as I kick, kick, kick.
M unch, munch, munch as I listen to Gilbert eat his breakfast.
Y eehaw! as me and Gilbert go galloping across the field.

W e went for a very long hack.
I love Gilbert, he makes me very happy.
T he hack made Gilbert hungry.
H e is the most handsomest gelding.
E xcuse me Gilbert I nearly fell off because you dropped your head.
R un, run, Gilbert, as fast as you can.
S crub-a-dub-dub, I scrubbed him with a sponge.

Tommy Withers (9)
Bolham Community Primary School, Bolham

I Am

I am as happy as a lion that gets its prey,
As happy as a pig that rolls in the mud all day.
As happy as a cat that has caught a mouse,
As happy as a spider running through the house.

I am as springy as a rabbit hopping down a hole,
As hungry as an owl about to eat a vole.
As busy as a bee collecting pollen on its knee,
As lazy as a sloth coolly sitting in a tree.

When you get to know me you will see,
All of these things are part of me.

I am a cheeky little boy who likes to have fun,
Chillin' with my dad, sis and mum.

Ruaridh Coutts (8)
Bolham Community Primary School, Bolham

Rock Hero

I am a Liverpool fan who wears the colour red,
I like to score goals, especially with my head.

When I score, I let out a roar,
The more I roar, the more I score.

I dream of being an F1 commentator as I'm its biggest fan,
I'll be the first autistic one, just to prove you can.

I'll be as famous as Murray Walker,
Because my mum says I'm a brilliant talker.

I will let you know who won the race,
With a massive smile upon my face.

Jenson Tarr (9)
Bolham Community Primary School, Bolham

What I Like And Who I Am

My name is Josh, I am very tall and my favourite game is football.
I like to run and play with my dog all day.
I live on a farm with cows and sheep and my dad has bees to keep.
I like to watch my dad and sister collect honey to make some money.
I have a rabbit named Molly and she is always jolly.
I have a dog named Sky who can run very fast and jump very high.
I have a dog named Sky just like the one up high.
My best dream of all is to be the very best at football.

Josh Reed (9)
Bolham Community Primary School, Bolham

All About Me

E xcited, I like to be excited about a lot of things,
that is also why my brain is making lots of
pings.
S inging is my favourite, making lots of noise, but
I also like buying new toys.
M iming, also known as acting, acting makes me
free, which also makes me feel like me!
E ducational, I love to learn at school, school
definitely beats chilling in some pool!

Esme Parker (9)

Bolham Community Primary School, Bolham

Rosie

Roses are red, violets are blue,
I can't wait for myself to bloom.

When it comes to maths, it gets confusing,
But the next day, I get it and I find it amusing.

My hair is curly and I am short,
And I am very slow but I'm good at sport.

I have blue eyes that like to shine,
And no one else has blue eyes just like mine.

Rosie Smith (8)
Bolham Community Primary School, Bolham

Me

'E llo, my name is Elliott B,
L ego and reading are great for me,
L essons at school are really fun,
I can't decide my favourite one,
O f course I like to have a big chat,
T hough I like cricket, I don't like to bat,
T his is the end of my acrostic verse,

B ye-bye!

Elliott Broadbent (9)
Bolham Community Primary School, Bolham

I Am Grateful For...

I am grateful for family and friends,
I love and am grateful for my pet Rubble.
For going to new places every day,
And for getting to be the best flower girl.
For having a lovely house,
For all the things I have.
All the clubs I have,
And the things I do.
I love my school,
And all of myself.

Holly Chappell (8)

Bolham Community Primary School, Bolham

William's Dreams

W ish I could be an engineer,
I like to make toys with gears.
L ove to watch F1 with my dad,
L ife without motorsport would be sad.
I have a dream,
A car that is green,
M y very own Formula 1 team.

William Walford (9)
Bolham Community Primary School, Bolham

I Love Horses

I love horses,
I ride courses,
I ride a horse called Tinker,
He is a very hard thinker,
He's very lazy,
I'm very gazy,
I'm also very hazy.

Poppy Alexander (9)
Bolham Community Primary School, Bolham

The Girl

A girl called Ava went to the store to buy food
Because she was starving and so was her mum
I am the kid
I am fast
I love to do art because I can paint
Also, I love animals and fruits
But I don't like to fly, it is boring
I have fun at the field trips because they are cool and awesome
I like to eat ice cream, it is yummy and tasty
I like to go outside to have fun and play tag and hide-and-seek
But I always get hurt some days
Also, I have fun at school at break and in maths
Because it is the best
I like to do English and French
I go outside to have fun and be excited
I am happy.

Humeyra Khan (8)
Delce Academy, Rochester

To Make Me You Need...

To make me you need...

Chicken nuggets McDonald's
A frog and monkey
Being good at maths, smart
Love
Football
Reading
PE
I'm happy and nosy.
Sweet and sour sauce
Love school
Love writing

And finally... I help a lot
And I'm nice.

Jack Allen (8)
Delce Academy, Rochester

This Is Me

I'm scared of spiders but I love animals
I do PE and I'm messy.
I'm a Jamaican girl but I'm fun
Don't worry if this will be done.
I love baking, I love art
I'm so smart
I'm brave and not a slave.
I'm also friendly,
I'm loud and I'm bakey.

Alexis-Rose Harrison (8)
Delce Academy, Rochester

All About Harry

I am as angry as King Kong.
I'm as silly as a bird.
I like football, I'm good at it.
I have a favourite team and it is called Liverpool.
I have skills in football like Salah.
I like playing on my Switch with my friends.
I am silly because I ran into a pole in my classroom.

Harry Stout (8)
Delce Academy, Rochester

All About Me!

A ctive me
L aughter and fun
L ove and care

A nd my mum
B rilliant
O ver the hill
U p the hill an ice cream van
T ravelling up the hill

M um gets me ice cream
E lectric scooter ride home.

Faith Davey (8)
Delce Academy, Rochester

This Is Me

T illy is my name,
H elping is my job,
I am a good helper,
S ometimes my friends help me,

I cheer my friends up,
S ometimes I don't play with my friends,

M y friends are great,
E veryone is my friend.

Tilly Fassum (8)
Delce Academy, Rochester

How To Make Me

You will need...
Fun
Disney and much more
Wait, I will tell you more!
Family, happiness, a pinch of fun
A bucket of art
Might as well add Fanta
Go on, add Disney
That's me for real
That's how to make me!

Millie Foster (8)
Delce Academy, Rochester

The Walking Dead

Once upon a time, I was walking in a city
Then I heard a noise
I looked out the window
Where everyone was playing bingo
Then I saw a zombie
It was coming for me
I tripped and I hurt my knee
The zombie got me on my knee!

Tyler-James Crew (7)
Delce Academy, Rochester

Fortnite And Football

My hair is as black as the night sky.
I am kind to all my friends.
I am as good as the world's best Fortnite player Bugha.
Rice is so yummy and healthy.
I am as good as Salah in football.

Artin Syla (8)
Delce Academy, Rochester

Christmas

Christmas is the best
It is messy because of the wrapping paper all over the floor
Cardboard boxes ripped.
The parents have a while to clean it up
The kids play upstairs with their toys.

Isla Turner (7)
Delce Academy, Rochester

Nice Niamh

Blue eyes, nice hair
I can be what I declare
I am also very fair
I am always aware
Art is my heart
I feel like I'm on a go-kart.

Niamh Fuller (8)
Delce Academy, Rochester

The Earth Is In Danger

The flowers turn into stone and
The grass turns into ash and
The trees are just sticks
The Earth is really in danger...

Reet Kaur Dhindsa (7)
Delce Academy, Rochester

Mystery Animal

I run with a herd.
I sleep in a barn.
I'm wild.
I'm light brown.
I go *neigh.*
What am I?

Grace Kimber (8)
Delce Academy, Rochester

Xbox One

I love to play my Xbox One
I am a banana skin
I am Spider-Man shooting webs from my hands
I love my Xbox One.

Alfie Hird (7)
Delce Academy, Rochester

My Fantastic Family

M y baby brother is very cute
Y et he can be quite mischievous

F or a one-year-old, my brother's very clever
A lso, I have a pet sausage dog named Rolo
N aughty yet adorable
T errific drawing is just one of my stepdad's skills
A nother is charming ladies
S ometimes my little sister annoys me a little bit
T hough she can be rather shouty, I love my mum
I f she's in a good mood, she brings lots of fun
C laire is her name

F ascinated by books, my dad is an author
A lso, he publishes and proofreads stories
M y stepmum has the same job as my dad
I love my fantastic family very much
L ife with my family is so great
Y et it could get even better...

Lucas Jones (9)
Mossley CE Primary School, Congleton

My Favourite Animal

My favourite animal has excellent night vision
My favourite animal has two lungs
My favourite animal can swim at a speed of 50km
My favourite animal can see colours that are not determined
My favourite animal goes to sleep with their eyes open
My favourite animal has a flattened skull
My favourite animal is quite slimy
My favourite animal eats bugs, grasshoppers, mealworms and more
My favourite animal in a group is called an 'army'
My favourite animal is allergic to fruit, human food, bright-coloured bugs and more
My favourite animal is most likely poisonous if they are a bright colour
My favourite animal can't live in the ocean or any saltwater
My favourite animal is most likely to be found in a pond or a lake

My favourite animal is an amphibian
My favourite animal has a scientific name called Anura

Answer: A fancy frog.

Megan Barnes (9)
Mossley CE Primary School, Congleton

About Me And My Unique Life

This is a poem including puzzles about my life,
Firstly, my country's flag is red, blue and white,
Its wonderful colours are crisscrossed left to right,
Another clue about my nationality is we are well-known for our fish and chips,
Come on! That was a huge clue, didn't all the clues click?
This is a poem including puzzles about my life,
Second, guess my loved passion,
I ride four-legged mammals - that wear some sort of fashion,
I've been doing this sport since I was three,
And when I ride, I feel free,
Have you got the hint?
Have you found the clue?
If you haven't, I'll be confused too,
This is a poem including puzzles about my life,

I also am quite unique,
Some would consider me a freak,
I hope this wasn't a bore,
Let me know if you want some more.

Freya Brown (10)
Mossley CE Primary School, Congleton

My Little Star

Something beautiful, sweet and cute,
Her fluff is as course as a bear's fur,
Her eyes glisten through the sun like a waterfall,
Her cries echo through my head like a microphone,
Her cute puppy eyes would constantly switch
through my head like a movie,
Her barks would fill my head with wonderful
thoughts,
It's like I can read what she's saying, like a
bookworm,
As I see her running around, I stare at the blue sky
as
I saw her face reflect in the sun,
The stars glistened in the midnight sky as I could
hear
A sweet whisper go through my ear,
She'll always be mine,
She'll always be here,
She'll always be my little star.

Luena Ritchie (10)
Mossley CE Primary School, Congleton

The Rhyming Eating Poem

Meatballs are small, beef is big,
It is all made from cows, not pigs.
Burgers are tasty, so are sweets,
They are my favourite treat.

Cheese is tasty on lots of things,
Eat it - that will make you a king.
Bananas are funny shaped, so are pears,
I still eat them, I don't care.

Pasta is my favourite food,
It gets me out of a grumpy mood.
You can eat pizza and use it in fractions,
It will make you a superhero in action.

My mum makes pies with all kinds of flavour,
You could ask her to make you one as a favour.
My tall dad eats lots of black pudding,
He eats so much it makes him look like a pudding.

George Bradley (10)
Mossley CE Primary School, Congleton

The Recipe Of Me

One cup of singing,
Half a cup of dancing,
A jug of happiness,
A bowl full of spending time with family and friends,
150g of humour,
Two bowls full of love,
A bowl and a half of kindness.

Steps to make me...
Add one cup of singing and half a cup of dancing to a bowl, then mix, mix, mix until bubbly.
Next, add a jug of happiness, a bowl of spending time with family and friends and 150g of humour.
Whisk until it looks like batter.
Mix two bowls of love and a bowl and a half of kindness until your heart is content.
Finally, sprinkle with joy and share.

Neesha Stingemore (9)
Mossley CE Primary School, Congleton

How To Make Me: My Recipe Book

First, add a sprinkle of fun in a bowl.
Secondly, add two handfuls of art.
Mix it in.
Third, add a tablespoon of purple paint.
Mix it in.
Next, add a dough full of India.
Use your hands and knead it in until you have a purple pigment.
After that, add a tad of Galaxy chocolate.
Mix it in.
Then add a pinch of family powder and spread it around the mix.
After you have done that, put your mix onto a doctor/helpful sheet.
Put it in the oven for seven minutes.
After that, take the mix out.
Then you have a helpful Olivia.
This is me!

Olivia Girish (9)
Mossley CE Primary School, Congleton

Zeeky Zac's Poem

Z eeky Zac,
A lways excited,
C razy dogs,
H ungry always,
A dore my Xbox.
R eady for the unexpected -
Y ummy food!

H appy most of the time,
E xplorer of the world.
N o annoying siblings,
N octurnal slightly,
A ssassin of wasps,
M ozarella stuffed crust pepperoni pizza is my favourite,

D angerous dinosaur obsessed,
A chy legs from swimming,
L over of dogs,
E xcuse user!

This is me, Zac.

Zachary Hennam-Dale (10)
Mossley CE Primary School, Congleton

In My World

This me, I am Sophie,
In the past, I had a pet fishie,
This is me, I animate and edit,
But don't worry, I don't take all the credit,
This is me, I love octopuses,
When it comes to travelling, I'm very curious,
This is me, my dream job is a writer,
And I was born mid-winter,
This is me, I really love art,
Don't worry, only my dog farts,
This is me, I have a pet cat,
And this cat ruins my mat,
This is me, I post letters and make it send,
That's my world, and this is the end.

Sophie McCall (10)
Mossley CE Primary School, Congleton

I Am Beatrix

My name is Beatrix, I love dogs
And my friend loves frogs
I don't really like to dance
I like the croissants made in France
My name is Beatrix, I love to be me
I'm sure if you were yourself, you'd be like me
Seven is my lucky number
My sister loves cucumber
I'm not that keen
I act like the Queen
My name is Beatrix
I love my family, my mum likes to bake
I normally eat all the cakes!
My name is Beatrix and...
This is me!

Beatrix Tonks (9)
Mossley CE Primary School, Congleton

This Is Me!

I ntelligent when it comes to writing,
S ometimes gaming,
A lways eating food,
B rilliant student,
E legant sometimes,
L oves my dog Bella and her hugs,
L ives in a cosy bedroom,
E very time I snooze, I lose,

W ears white comfy shoes,
A lways snoozing in my bed,
R ather wear comfy clothes than fancy ones!
E ats sweets all day.

This is Isabelle Ware.

Isabelle Ware (9)
Mossley CE Primary School, Congleton

I'm A Fabulous Child

My name is Riley and I like to game
My favourite game is Fortnite and it's fun to play
I'm a fabulous child because I always go wild
I want Covid to end so we can finally have some fun
And I also like to run
This poem's about me
I hate when I get stung by a bee
I also like football
Because I get to kick a ball
I also like basketball
Because it uses an orange ball
I am a fabulous child
Especially because I can run a mile.

Riley Hamnett (10)
Mossley CE Primary School, Congleton

Something About Me

S uper good at video games
T ornadoes are cool I think
U ntidy people really need to clean
F un at games
F ishing is very fun I think

A little rascal
B est at running races
O utside is my favourite place to play
U njoyful people are the type of people I help
T he type of drawings I do are cartoons

M ason is my name
E njoying football is very easy.

Mason Stubbs (9)
Mossley CE Primary School, Congleton

How To Make Me!

Ingredients
Animal adorer
Crazy chocoholic
Bonkers Bookworm
Guitar lover
As friendly as a delightful dog
As funny as a feline
As sweet as sugar
A giant spoon of cheesy macaroni

Method
Mix as friendly as a delightful dog and as funny as a feline,
Add crazy chocoholic and bonkers bookworm.
Decorate with some guitar love
But don't forget sugar, animal spice and macaroni.

This is me!

Erin Frost (10)
Mossley CE Primary School, Congleton

I Am Arthur

A nnoying to my brother and sister
R apid at running
T hankful for food
H appy all the time
U nique in my own way
R estless at everything

H ungry for food
I ndividual - a lone wolf
B ouncy, I jump a lot
B alls. I like to play in ball pits
E xcited for my birthday
R ummaging for toys
T rickster. Pull out jokes!

This is me!

Arthur Hibbert (10)
Mossley CE Primary School, Congleton

A Mixture Of Me

There is nothing like a good book,
I love it when I feel shook.
I'm so into animals,
Just not really camels.
When I play netball, I run like a dog,
But when I'm trampolining, I hop like a frog.
A fun fact is that it's hard being smart,
To make it equal, I often do art.
Friends and family make me happy,
My little sister loves to be clappy.
The main thing is having fun,
It makes me as toasty as a hot cross bun.

Sadie Brownsword (9)
Mossley CE Primary School, Congleton

How To Make Me...

You will need a bag of fun,
A bag of Marvel,
A pinch of singing,
A twinkle of dancing,
A bunch of love and family,
A bunch of friends,
A bag of Alton Towers,
A handful of Disney World,
You will need to crack the fun egg, then the bag of Marvel, then sing,
Mix it well up, put dancing in,
Then love and family, then the friends,
Alton Towers, then Disney,
Mix, bake, then you will have me.

This is me.

Connie Eardley (9)
Mossley CE Primary School, Congleton

My Favourite Animal Ever!

My favourite animal does not live in the sky and
doesn't like to say hi.
It uses its camo and is not shot by soldiers with
ammo.
It has nine brains and has never seen a train.
It has a beak in-between its eight legs and does
not use treads.
Its jet propulsion makes it faster than a shark, but
it can't go to the park.
It has two eyes and has never had pie.

My favourite animal is an octopus!
I wonder if you guessed it.

Jin Sugano-Kirkham (9)
Mossley CE Primary School, Congleton

How To Make Me

Ingredients:
A pinch of sport,
Ten grams of happiness,
A drop of annoyance,
A bag of V-Bucks,
And a hundred books.

Recipe:
First, get your batter and add a pinch of sport with a drop of annoyance.
Then add ten grams of happiness and a hundred books and start to mix.
After that, put it in the oven for thirty minutes and play Fortnite.
Finally, take it out the oven and sprinkle V-Bucks on.

Freddie Garnsey (10)
Mossley CE Primary School, Congleton

My Name Is...

T ommy is my name, as you can see.
O nce, I tried to skip PE.
M y favourite animal is a dog.
M y favourite green slimy animal is a frog.
Y o-yos are ultra cool.

B ut I'd prefer a swimming pool.
A re you still there?
R abbits have a bunch of hair.
L ucas is my friend.
O nce, me and my brother ran away from hens.
W ell, that is the end.

Tommy Barlow (10)
Mossley CE Primary School, Congleton

What Makes Me, Me!

W onderfully funny,
H appy all the time,
A nimals for days,
T ons of laughter,

M otivated,
A wesome art,
K ind,
E xtremely loveable,
S uperb smiling,

C aring hands,
H uggable,
L ike a dolphin, I speed through the water,
O wns two crazy rats,
E njoys spending time with my family and friends.

Chloe Longshaw (10)
Mossley CE Primary School, Congleton

Facts About Me!

My name is Freya
My favourite animal is a tiger
And my twin brother likes apple cider.
My favourite colour is purple
And my cousin's favourite animal is a turtle.

My name is Freya
I have three cats
And they like to chase bats.
I love to play on the keyboard
And my brother likes to play with swords.

My name is Freya
I love to have fun
And my friends like relaxing in the sun.

Freya Garnsey (10)
Mossley CE Primary School, Congleton

This Is Myself

T ea drinker with a yummy, tasty chocolate biscuit.
H ates mean bullies but loves kind friends.
I s very happy when playing with my friendly, fluffy dog.
S its still when I need to.

I sn't rude at all, even when someone is mean.
S ings favourite songs but not always.

M assive hot chocolate drinker.
E ats favourite foods like pasta, and ice cream too.

Renae Darlington (9)
Mossley CE Primary School, Congleton

Why I'm Unique!

W hen I go to see my family, I have so much fun.
H appy most of the time.
Y es, I like gaming.

I like football.
M y name is Charlie Cook.

U nlike netball, I like hockey.
N o one can beat my hero, Mo Salah.
I have a lovely family.
Q uick but not as fast as my friends
U sually I'm funny.
E very Friday I do cricket.

Charlie Cook (10)
Mossley CE Primary School, Congleton

My Unique Self!

My life is mine,
To make everything divine,
To brighten up your day,
To make you stay,
To fill you full of love and joy,
From each girl to each boy,
A pinch of musical talent and beats,
A helping hero,
Always interested in science since I was zero,
Absolutely loves books,
Loves to explore in nooks,
I love to bake,
I love the cake,
My name is Sienna and,
This is my unique self!

Sienna Boorsma-Dyson (10)
Mossley CE Primary School, Congleton

This Is Cailin Tomlin's Life

T urtles are one of my favourite animals
H orses are my world
I am a flexible gymnast
S low freestyle and contemporary are my
favourite types of dancing that I do

I adopt a share of multiple horses and ponies
S leeping makes me calm

M y dream is to become an Olympic horse rider or
a horse riding teacher
E lephants are my favourite zoo animals.

Cailin Tomlins (9)

Mossley CE Primary School, Congleton

My Best Friend Blaze

Sunday is my favourite day because I get to see my best friend Blaze,
When I pass, he's eating grass and wants a treat to eat,
In my dreams, he's galloping round the field all day, neighing to his friends, "Hey!"
I can't wait for this virus to be done with so I can go to the stables and have some fun,
And my friend Blaze will be waiting with a head full of hay,
Excited in bed where he lay.

Holly Clack (10)
Mossley CE Primary School, Congleton

This Is My Life

T he beautiful sounds of the TV,
H earing the birds tweeting,
I n the peaceful, calm country Wales,
S tarting to get hungry,

I nside my tummy,
S coring lots of goals,

M ithering to get the boat out,
Y anking the joy,

L oving my Xbox,
I n the house,
F ishing in the boat,
E nding the poem.

Max Hillier (9)
Mossley CE Primary School, Congleton

My Beautiful Self

O pen-minded in scientific facts
W riter of English and maths
E xcited eater of margarita pizza
N ot a nuisance in most things

S cience lover forever
I ncredible in a lot of things
M usician
P asta scoffer (with any sauce)
S ongwriter
O utside player for goalkeeping
N ever complain (unless I'm tired).

Owen Simpson (10)
Mossley CE Primary School, Congleton

I Am Ellie!

My name's Ellie
I love to have fun
My best friend's Beatrix
And she likes dogs.
We sit on logs and talk about frogs,

I like to play football with my friend Holly
And she seems so jolly

I like to go to the cinema with my friend Sienna
And like to watch Friends with fries in my hand

My name's Ellie and...
This is me!

Ellie Cartwright (9)
Mossley CE Primary School, Congleton

This Is Me

T ea drinker with milky chocolate biscuit
H uge hugs for best friends
I s adventurous with Nanny and Grandad on rope swing
S illy and crazy with annoying brother

I s very pretty as a rainbow can be
S illy like my kind mother

M assive milky chocolate lover
d **E** ep walker, dreamer, sleeper.

Isabelle Roberts (10)
Mossley CE Primary School, Congleton

The Ingredients That Make Me

I don't know where to start,
All I know is I love art.
I also like animals,
Especially mammals.
I'm very good at gymnastics,
And I adore Tangfastics.
Spending time with friends and family makes me ecstatic,
I enjoy it so much, I don't hide in the attic.
The main thing is having fun,
And celebrating the fact that you have won.

Sophie Austen (10)
Mossley CE Primary School, Congleton

On My Planet

This is me, I'm Mia,
In the past, I used to have two dogs,
I'm really good at reading,
I love music,
This is me, I love horses,
When it comes to exploring, I'm very careful,
This is me, my daydream is to become a horse rider,
I love biking and I would do more riding,
I adopted four Shetland ponies,
They are real homies!

Mia Taylor (10)
Mossley CE Primary School, Congleton

I Am Unique

I love my family so much,

A kind, nice person,
M ade to be good.

U nderstanding everything in my way,
N obody is the same as me,
I n the zone for video games,
Q uick, I am very quick,
U nique like everyone is,
E ats pizza,

This is me!

Toby Law (9)
Mossley CE Primary School, Congleton

I Am Unique

T he things that make me unique are the things that I like.
H elpful and a great friend.
I love fish and puppies.
S wimming and basketball.

I like football.
S hrek.

M y favourite thing to do is play with my friends and on my Xbox.
E xcited to go on holiday.

Oscar Juggins-Stewart (10)
Mossley CE Primary School, Congleton

This Is Me

You will need
A bedroom full of sewing stuff
A netball hoop
A rugby ground
Sweet strawberries

Instructions
Mix a bedroom full of sewing stuff
And a netball hoop together.

Add a rugby ground and seven sweet
Strawberries to the mixture and bake for
Thirty minutes.
This is me.

Jessica Cashmore (10)
Mossley CE Primary School, Congleton

This Is Me

J olly all the time,
A happy person,
K arate isn't my favourite,
E mbarrassing for my family!

A lot of the time happy,
U nhappy sometimes,
B ored sometimes,
E mbarrassing to my cousin!
R unner,
T raining to be a footballer.

Jake Aubert (9)
Mossley CE Primary School, Congleton

This Is Me!

T his is me...
H elpful to others
I am as cute as a koala bear...
S o come play with me, I will share

I am as cuddly as a sloth...
S o come cuddle me, I am as soft as a cloth

M akes amazing chocolate brownies
E mma is my name and this is me!

Emma Nicholas-Norbury (9)
Mossley CE Primary School, Congleton

I Am Charlie!

C ricket and football lover,
H ilarious and funny,
A wesome apple devourer,
R hyming jokester,
L aughing lover,
I nspiring,
E xciting eater,

G reedy food lover,
I maginary dreamer,
L ovely hard worker,
L olly licker.

Charlie Gill (10)
Mossley CE Primary School, Congleton

Hi, My Name Is Eva

My name is Eva,
I like horse riding,
I ride a horse called Fudge,
Sometimes he likes hiding.
I like lying with my dog,
In the park he chases frogs.
I like drawing blueprints,
I like eating yummy Polo mints.
My favourite film is Black Beauty,
Black horses are all cute.
My name is Eva.

Eva McCdenton (9)
Mossley CE Primary School, Congleton

How To Be You...

H appy powers,
A sprinkle of joy,
P eacefulness,
P henomenally a bit of individual parts,
I ntelligent, everlasting love,
N obleness,
E ven laughter,
S uperb happiness (a bundle of it)
S uperpowers.

Callum French (9)
Mossley CE Primary School, Congleton

This Is Me

To make me
You need:
A gallon of talent
A tub of friends
A bit of laziness
A cup of laughter
A spoonful of annoyance
And perhaps one more bit
Then to finish, a serving
of all of them again.

Jack Blench (10)
Mossley CE Primary School, Congleton

The Poem About My Life

A kennings poem

I am a...

Chocolate devourer,
Animal lover,
Peanut butter on toast chomper,
Soft teddy snuggler,
Sweet beggar,
Book reader,
Raspberry guzzler,
Freezing ice cream licker.
This is me.

Bethan Wright (10)
Mossley CE Primary School, Congleton

The Poem Of Me

A kennings poem

I am a...
Book reader
Dog whisperer
FIFA rager
Sweets consumer
Tired riser
Unlucky trier
Football fanatic
Birdie basher
Corky smasher
And finally...
A great, great helper.

Lucas Worthy (10)
Mossley CE Primary School, Congleton

Daniel

D ips chips in ketchup,
e **A** ts mint Aeros,
e **N** joys playing games on my iPad,
I like watching YouTube,
E nergetic,
L aughs a lot,

This is me!

Daniel Howard (9)
Mossley CE Primary School, Congleton

What I Am

I am,
As brave as a tiger,
I am as strong as a lion,
I punch like Mike Tyson,
I love all my family,
I support the best team, Liverpool FC,
This is me!

Mason Smith (9)
Mossley CE Primary School, Congleton

My Favourite Things

M y dog Tess has great eyebrows, a tail too,
Y ellow is my favourite colour, but not blue.

F oods I love are lemons and limes,
A nd I like cuddling my teddy bear at all times.
V ery fluffy socks make my feet warm,
O h, I forgot to tell you, they also make me yawn.
U ntil now I didn't like chilli con carne for tea,
R ecently I love it and I think you'd agree.
I like making hama beads in my room,
T oday I designed a new costume,
E very day in spring I see new flowers bloom.

T he best things I like to eat are just out of reach,
H appily, I can still go to the beach.
I like to eat Galaxy bars,
N ow and then I look up at the stars.
G oing to my theatre group where everyone sings,
S o now you know all my favourite things.

Alice Hitchins (8)
Notting Hill & Ealing Junior School, Ealing

This Is Me

This poem is about me, my name is Layla,
I'm ten years old with a younger sister called Maya.
I live in West Ealing, very near to my school,
It's not far to walk which makes it quite cool.
I love all my lessons, but maths is my favourite,
As I like problem-solving, I just have a taste for it.
I enjoy playing sports: netball, hockey and swimming,
It's great being in a team, especially when you're winning.
With four operations, I've had to be brave and resilient.
I'm surrounded by amazing friends who are just brilliant.
I have a dog called Ralph with silky red fur,
He goes crazy for squirrels wherever they stir.
My grandparents are called Jido and Teta,
They spoil me with treats and let me stay up later.
My mummy is a dentist who looks after people's teeth,
"Open wide," she says as they look up, hiding their grief.

And Daddy does something on his laptop all day,
No one knows what exactly as he tap-taps away.
My little sister Maya loves playing lots of games,
Her favourite is chess where she wins all the
frames.
So that's about it, my life summed up on a page,
My journey so far, at least up to this stage.
I'm excited about what the future may bring,
If it involves fun and laughter, my heart will sing.

Layla Richardson (10)
Notting Hill & Ealing Junior School, Ealing

All About Me

I'm friendly and curious, that's how I like to be.
I draw on the beach when the sun shines out to sea.
I stare at the meadows when daisies bloom in spring.
Being kind and polite makes me feel bright.
Pasta is my favourite meal, I have it every week.
And sometimes when I'm feeling brave, I go outside to seek.
I enjoy painting with my colours, we hang my pictures on the wall.
Shining high up, standing nice and tall.
Writing in my diary at the end of the day, all about the fun I had with lots and lots of play.
When I rest my head at night, I look up at the stars.
Thoughts of what tomorrow brings, everyone might gently sing.
Rabbits hop in summer, under the warm golden sun.
While everyone is laughing, having lots of fun.
I feel curious and courageous, but sometimes I'm outrageous.

Skipping and dancing, off I go.
Building snowmen in the cold white snow.
Christmas is my favourite, watching movies all day long.
Then my birthday comes around and we make lots of sound, friends and family gather round.
This is *me!*

Ariana Ladwa (9)
Notting Hill & Ealing Junior School, Ealing

K-A-I-R-A

That is how you spell my name,
Always ready to try new things,
Dancing, jumping and singing,
I'm very creative,
Making arts and crafts,
Shooting in archery and playing with darts,
Always got my nose stuck in a book,
If you've got a good one, I'll come and take a look!
Flying in a rocket to the moon,
Winning a horse race very, very soon,
Jumping, writing, walking,
Laughing, joking and talking.
Shooting a goal in netball,
Or playing football.

An imagination as wild as fire,
Which sometimes leads to fear,
But I always feel better when my parents are near,
When I'm sad, I'll think of something good,
Express my emotions as everyone should,
Travelling on an aeroplane,
Or sitting in a bus or train.

Silk hair, purple glasses,
Here is a list of my favourite classes:
Science, maths and history,
I'll try and solve any mystery,
I'll never give up,
Adore all animals from bears to pups,
This is my poem all about me,
If you're interested, come and see!

Kaira Agarwal Dora (9)

Notting Hill & Ealing Junior School, Ealing

I'm Just A Person

I'm just a person,
I'm just a student,
No good at German,
I don't do what I shouldn't,
I'm glad that's how they think...

For really, what I do,
Will blow your mind away,
You should really take a seat and listen to,
What I did today...

First, I woke up as usually people would,
Then I went to have a shower as usually people *should*,
After that, I went to see the snacks Mum had packed for school,
And switched the celery for a packet of crisps,
Mum wouldn't mind... Anyway, if I hadn't done that
I would've thrown it in the pool!

Once I got to school,
I got a football,

I went to the back of the playground,
And started kicking it around.

I ate my crisps at break,
And sneakily escaped,
Through the gates,
Surely it was fine to miss *one* school day...

So I'm still a person,
I'm still a student,
I'm still no good at German,
And that is how I'll stay...

Amelia Farooqi (10)
Notting Hill & Ealing Junior School, Ealing

Me!

Supersonic netballer,
Shoot-into-a-hoop scorer,
Dance like you just don't care,
Wave your pink hair in the air,
Hang out with my nutty friends,
With me, the fun just never ends,
Laugh until you can't laugh anymore,
Wanna go skateboarding? Okay, sure,
So now you see,
What it's like being me.

She's tall enough to touch the clouds,
She dances so she wows the crowds,
She really likes cats, they're her favourite animal,
Watch her play violin in her string ensemble,
Kassie and her play all day every day,
They always find a new imaginary game to play,
She loves telling jokes, every day they get funnier,
Who's this awesome person? Her name is Olivia!

I love space.
My most favourite planet's *name* is Saturn.
It *means* God of Agriculture!
I love cats.
I *have* two.
Bluebell has *dignity.*
Bramble is feisty.
(Look at every four words).

Olivia Sherman (10)

Notting Hill & Ealing Junior School, Ealing

Awesomeness

W e can work together to make a big change,
E veryone cares for each other,

A ll of us are awesome,
R ain is more fun than wind because it makes puddles which are fun,
E verybody can try their best,

G ardeners grow flowers as beautiful as the Northern Lights in their gardens,
R abbits are furry, fluffy, small, different-coloured and last of all, super cute,
E ach and every one of us is unique in our own ways, so be proud,
A ct your very best to spread joy around,
T hank people for doing something kind to make them happy.

P uppies lick you and are as playful as children,
E fforts are always worth it in the end,
O ften, other people think they can't do things when they can,
P laying is fun when you are fair to each other,
L ove your family and friends,
E njoy the company of the nice people around you.

Cordelia Chuang (7)
Notting Hill & Ealing Junior School, Ealing

Annika's Perfect Pudding

Ingredients
- A cute cup of kindness
- A cub scarf
- Risk
- Care
- Your heart that is larger than life
- Patience and sensitivity
- A tough of magic
- Half a dozen guitar strings

Gentle warning!
This recipe takes patience and sensitivity...

Preheat the oven to a calm, caring setting.
Add the cute cup of kindness and half a dozen guitar strings.
Next, stir with a touch of magic, which of course I love to do.
Pour in a generous amount of your heart that is larger than life.
Don't forget to slowly add risk with lots of care.
Make sure to leave it to rest with your cub scarf, this makes it nice and fluffy.

After ten to fifteen minutes, you can place your creation in the oven with tender, loving control. There you have it, 'Annika's perfect pudding'.

P.S. Make sure to smell the aroma of happiness!

Annika Aggarwal (9)
Notting Hill & Ealing Junior School, Ealing

Ballet Dreams

I love ballet and I know it is true
The world seems so different and I'm no longer blue
The world seems to smile as I spin on the spot
And all the time that I use seems to come to a stop
I don't need to think as I leap and I bound
All dressed in pink as I go round and round

Sugar Plum Fairy, princess or mouse
I become what I see as I dance in my house
I'll become you and you become me
'Cause there's no limit to what a dancer can be
As I jump to the ground and become a Tudor while being crowned
And my parents applaud with a deafening sound
I am no longer me, funny Lydie
But I am the queen of my fantasy

I can't wait to be famous and go on a tour
And be the person who people adore

I will be better than Anna Pavlova
And dance on stage going further than Russia

That is my dream
That is my dream.

Lydie Vladimery (9)
Notting Hill & Ealing Junior School, Ealing

Solo My Cat

My cat, my cat,
As cheeky as a rat,
He's king of the house,
He loves to eat a mouse.

He will play, he will play,
Whenever there's day,
With energetic jumps,
And occasional bumps.

Though when stuff's mysterious,
He's deadly serious,
Sniffing the air,
Like something's out there.

As soon as the day's out,
The time of no shout,
He's on the bed,
Like he has fled,
The life of outside,
Where he travels far and wide.

When meows are heard,
He'll be catching a bird,
Or waiting at the front door,
Firm on the floor.

His enemies he fights,
At all different heights,
Yet sometimes he flees,
Hiding behind the trees.

Solo the cat,
Acts like a rat,
Head of the house,
Loves to eat a mouse.

Martha Bramhall (10)
Notting Hill & Ealing Junior School, Ealing

Amatullah

A rtistic like Van Gogh and always experimenting with arts and crafts
M agical with her hands, creating origami pieces and persevering when a fold goes wrong
A ctive in sports and believes anything is possible
T rue to every promise and loyal to a fault
U nderstands the emotions of other people
L ike a rainbow, she adds colour to each gloomy day
L oves to play with little children and make them laugh
A lways cheering on her friends and finding joy in their achievements
H umble at a netball match while congratulating the opposing team

Amatullah is
A mazing,
M emorable,
A rticulate,
T rustworthy,
U nique,
L oving,
L oyal
A nd
H appy.

Amatullah Abidali (10)
Notting Hill & Ealing Junior School, Ealing

Pleased To Meet You

'The Roman Mysteries' are my favourite books,
In my free time, I bake and cook.
From the rainbow, I'd choose blue,
I don't like buckles on my shoe.
Tap dance, street dance, even hip-hop,
Watch me groove and see me bop!
A dog would be my number one pet,
I would teach it the Greek alphabet.
Whenever I can, I watch TV,
My preferred channel is CBBC.
I adore playing cricket,
It feels good to take a wicket!
The best food ever is a chocolate bar,
And in football I support QPR!
Giraffes I love with their necks so long,
'Head and Heart' is my favourite song.
Spiders are, by far, my worst fear,
Other than that, I am filled with cheer.
A doctor I would love to be,
I hope you like this poem about me.

Sophia Hirachand (9)
Notting Hill & Ealing Junior School, Ealing

My Amazing Self

A nnabel Harley, that's my name,
N ot being naughty, that's my game.
N ice and easy mathematics I find.
A wesome I am, and brave and kind.
B lue like my glasses all nice and bright.
E verybody, need help? I'm useful all right.
L ove my family, that is me.

V ery best food is a Polo, not a green pea.

M ost favourite animal is a dinosaur,

H obbies are Lego plus reading and more.
A musement parks are my favourite day out,
R ides and treats are a really good shout,
L adders plus ropes, I'm having a good time,
E nergetic and fast, I love to climb.
Y ou now know all about my... amazing self!

Annabel Harley (8)
Notting Hill & Ealing Junior School, Ealing

This Is Me!

If I was able to have one special ability in the world
It would be to talk to babies
To understand how they feel and how they view the world
What they think is happening around them
Now I am a girl I can communicate when I am frustrated, lonely, excited and amazed, using my tone, voice and words.
When I am a woman, I might lose the sense of what it was like to feel emotions as girls and babies do
When I was a baby, I could not voice any of my feelings and could only display them.
If I can describe my feelings, do I still feel them in the same way?
So if I could talk to babies, then I could help them comprehend what is going on around them in the wide world.
And feel emotions again that time and age have made me forget.

Nalini Wilde (9)
Notting Hill & Ealing Junior School, Ealing

This Is Me, A Girl With Curly Hair

This is me, a girl with curly hair,
Which swirls and twirls and causes complete havoc in the air!
Some people love it, some people hate it, and some mornings,
I just can't face it!

Each strand twizzles and wiggles and tangles,
And the curls loop and coil like they're caught in a bangle!
Some days my hair is just plain old silly,
And other times it makes me feel quite dizzy!

'Wash hair' nights are the worst.
It starts off good, we wet it with water and it all calms down.
But then slowly but surely, all the curls come back and one by one they go *ping!*
Then *boing!*
And before I know it, we're back to square one!
This is me, a girl with curly hair!

Millie Bakstad (9)
Notting Hill & Ealing Junior School, Ealing

How To Create Me - This Is Me

In order to create me, you must add...
A toy-filled bedroom
A broken hairband
One tablespoon of talkativeness
One and a half tablespoons of fun
Five cups of happiness
A bowl of cup noodles
A splash of milk
A sprinkle of a sister's hair strand

Now you need to...
Add the toy-filled bedroom and the sprinkle of a sister's hair strand
Mix while adding five cups of happiness and a splash of milk
Keep mixing while adding one and a half tablespoons of fun
Add the one tablespoon of talkativeness, a broken hairband and stir

Add the bowl of cup noodles and fully cover with baking paper
Bake in oven for 30-45 minutes and then leave it to cool for 15 minutes.

Mylene Wang (10)
Notting Hill & Ealing Junior School, Ealing

All About Me

To make me, add some TV,
I have all kinds of smiles,
And I love my family.

I am a bit cheeky,
I eat lots of sugar,
I love all my sweeties,
I *don't* eat my boogers!

I am a big sister,
To a little brother called Reece,
His nickname is Mr,
In my life, he's a big piece.

I'm bad at Sudoku,
I love to go swimming,
I'm part of the cheeky crew,
In gymnastics, I'm winning.

My smiley pink cheeks,
Are as bright as candyfloss,
They make me unique,
Along with my gold hair, I like to toss.

The topic was me,
And that's all you need to know,
Now I'm intrigued,
It is your go.

Lauren Mankoo (9)
Notting Hill & Ealing Junior School, Ealing

This Is Me

This is me
Running all day long
Singing and winning until dawn comes along
I like to be my own strong match

I'm not ordinary, I'm extraordinary
In the spotlight, singing like a star
Night and day
Like a sunlight ray

I'm in the spotlight in the dark night
The crowd is screaming with delight
'Cause I am singing with all my might
This is me

I like to be my own stereo
In my world, I'm the greatest hero
Although in life there are some blank spaces, good and evil
I never lose hope

This is the real me
No costumes, no covers, no acts
Confident, kind, sporty and musical
This is me.

Aashi Morjaria (10)
Notting Hill & Ealing Junior School, Ealing

This Is Who I Am

I am just writing
About me, something exciting
This is who I am:
I really love cats
I have a cute one called Hank
This is what I love
Oh, I like to draw
Just to sketch with a pencil
This is what I do
Coding is my thing
I just love to make fun games
This is what I like
Wow, inspiration!
I imagine stories
This is how I think
I am quite funny
Laughing at jokes someone told
This is how I am
Science is epic
It is just fascinating
This is what I think

I have lots of friends
We are all pretty crazy
This is who we are
I am just ending
This poem I am writing
This is me, just Tess.

Tess Nathan (10)
Notting Hill & Ealing Junior School, Ealing

I Am

I am a slim, strong, sporty girl,
And my long silky hair has many curls

I am a granddaughter, a sister and a daughter,
And the unity in my family makes us stronger

I am a dreamer with great aspirations,
And one day, I will be swimming in the crystal ocean

I run as fast as a cheetah,
And enjoy eating pasta and pizza

I am a talented netball shooter,
And a brilliant football striker

I am adventurous and enjoy travelling,
And every country I visit is another blessing

I am determined to make the world more organic,
And now I always avoid using plastic

This is me and I am on top of the world!

Nina Jaffer (9)
Notting Hill & Ealing Junior School, Ealing

If In Doubt...

My motto is: 'If in doubt, read a book!'

When feeling sad and a little bit down,
Stories about animals erase my frown.

When I want to travel, but there's nowhere to go,
I jump into a tale of a long time ago.

Turning the pages makes my worries disappear,
When the villain is defeated, I let out a great cheer!

When my tummy is rumbling and I need something quick,
Through my favourite cookbook I can flick.

Whatever kind of day I've had, you see,
Reading really does set my mind free.

So my advice to you is, "If in doubt, read a book!"

Ella Chow (10)
Notting Hill & Ealing Junior School, Ealing

Myself, Inside Out To Outside In

Dog lover,
Book reader,
Nintendo player,
Football fan,
Thrilling table tennis,
Tough but fun
Lego technic,
Cricket king,
Stapler liker,
Guitar god,
Terrific tennis,
Tremendous like TinTin,
Fun friend,
Good in golf,
Calvin and Hobbes liker,
Magnificent M&M's,
Amazing mac 'n' cheese,
Super Spain,
Cracking Costa Rica,

Incredible India,
Marvellous Maldives,
Superb Stevie Nicks,
Jumping Joan Jett,
Dashing David Gilmour,
Brilliant B. B. King,
Exciting Eric Clapton,
Majestic Manchester United,
Dare to dream to have my own band.

Mehr Arora (9)
Notting Hill & Ealing Junior School, Ealing

Determined

I begin with a 'D' and end with a 'D',
You may never imagine the things I might be,
I may look some weak, but I am nothing but strong,
My life's the lyrics to a never-ending song.

When the weight on my shoulders reaches up high,
I never give up, I will never show why,
Ever-existent problems shake up my life,
I turn to these ten letters that fill me with strife.

As mighty as a lion that roars in the wind,
I'll always be a fighter, I'll never give in,
Where there's darkness, really there is a light,
I will always be determined and do what's right.

Agnès Fanthorpe Collings (10)
Notting Hill & Ealing Junior School, Ealing

Me!

My name is Amaya,
I am ten years old,
I love a meal,
And have a heart of gold,
I hope you appreciate getting to know me,
Let me introduce you to my family,
Mother, Father, brother and of course me,
There are many things I like to do,
Reading, art, cycling and some sports too,
What's special to me you will definitely find,
Family, friends, school and to retain a sharp mind,
I hope to help people and be a doctor someday,
And to go to some of the best universities along the way,
Now we must end, we have run out of time,
Thank you, thank you, the pleasure is all mine!

Amaya Parmar (10)
Notting Hill & Ealing Junior School, Ealing

What I Do

I'm a girl who's not like the rest,
I'm not the worst girl, nor the best.
I often imagine a world so clean,
Without global warming or Covid-19.
I imagine this world that could never be,
Then I imagine this world the way I see.
On Saturdays and Sundays I like to play games,
I'm the only one who has my special name.
I like to read for hours on end,
And sometimes singing, well, that depends.
Ding! Ding! Oh look at the time!
I hope you enjoyed this wonderful rhyme!
Ring! Ring! Oh no! Just look at the time!
Well, I've got to leave, goodbye!

Yeeting Gao (9)
Notting Hill & Ealing Junior School, Ealing

This Is Me, Chloe

T he name is Chloe. The age is nine.
H ow are you doing? I'm just fine.
I s your favourite colour red? Mine is too.
S econd favourite colour though is probably blue.

I gloos are too cold.
S unshine is too hot.

M y life is full of being picky quite a lot.
E veryone thinks I'm quite nuts.

C os I'm always having too much fun.
H appy I am always. Day and night.
L oving cats was always part of my life.
O nly if you do know me well.
E ternity, forever friends we will be.

Chloe Lee (9)
Notting Hill & Ealing Junior School, Ealing

My Hopes And Dreams For The Future

I know right now I am a little girl
But I have big dreams and hopes
For what happens in the world

When I grow up, I want to write
I think that through my writing
I will help the world be bright

My personality is strong
I care about the world, people, animals and plants
I know the difference between right and wrong

In my stories and books
I will encourage the good and discourage the bad
We must judge by our actions, not our looks

I'd like my books to inspire
I want good to come from them
And make the world's expectations higher.

Annalise Hughes-Jarvis (9)
Notting Hill & Ealing Junior School, Ealing

How To Make Me

You will need:

A pinch of **M** ischief
3 grams of **I** nspiration
10 cuddly **S** loths
1 litre of **H** appiness
1 tsp of **A** thleticism
10 litres of **L** aughter

Mix in a big glass bowl with:

1 cup of good **B** ehaviour
1kg of **H** ilarity
5 juicy **A** pples
2 tsp of **T** alkative
500ml of **T** alent
Bags of **E** nergy
A ton of **E** nthusiasm

Put into the mould and bake for
1 hour at 200 degrees celsius in a
pre-heated oven.
Let it cool down and then
enjoy a little piece of me!

Mishal Bhattee (9)
Notting Hill & Ealing Junior School, Ealing

This Is Like Me

The wind through the air,
As light as my hair,
This is like me, like me.

The branches like pegs,
As strong as my legs,
This is like me, like me.

Stars pierce the sky,
As bright as my eyes,
This is like me, like me.

A hungry cat hears,
As keen as my ears,
This is like me, like me.

A great speeding train,
As quick as my brain,
This is like me, like me.

A big strawberry tart,
As nice as my heart,
This is like me, like me.

Playing with friends,
My joy never ends,
This is all me, all me!

Zoe Trisk (9)

Notting Hill & Ealing Junior School, Ealing

Delicious, Dazzling Daya

Introduction
Follow these instructions to see how Daya is made up.

Ingredients
Funny, cheeky
Caring, clever
Competitiveness, confidence
Strong, happiness
Small

Method
Add 100g of fabulous funny into a bowl.
Then add a cup of caring and competitiveness.
After, stir in 2 tablespoons of strong and small.
Mix a pinch of cheeky and a dash of clever.
Penultimately, throw in 25ml of confidence.
Finally, sprinkle a teaspoon of happiness.

This will make delicious Daya,
Enjoy with friends and family.

Daya Nanda (8)
Notting Hill & Ealing Junior School, Ealing

Things I Like To Do

I like to be polite
I love to make arts and crafts, the ideas pop into my head
I love to make people's frowns upside down so they have the best emotion
Happy!

Playing with my youngest cousins is my favourite thing to do
I give them stickers to make them happy and give them tattoos too
I love to make new friends, it is the best thing I can do

I like to reuse things like cups...
At the end of the day, it's movie night
The best thing is the popcorn, my favourite is sweet and salty
And that's the end of the things I like to do.

Lubna Al-Jibouri (7)
Notting Hill & Ealing Junior School, Ealing

Reflections Of Me

When I look in the mirror
What do I see?
An eight-year-old girl
Staring back at me.

I have long curly hair
And eyes shot with gold.
I'm good at school
And do what I am told.

I like dancing and singing,
I'm good at art and craft.
Sometimes I'm serious
And sometimes I am daft.

When I grow up
I want to be an author.
Maybe one day
I'll even have a daughter.

It's time to go to school,
Mummy's brushing my hair.
Today I'll do my work
With lots and lots of care.

Josephine Churley (8)

Notting Hill & Ealing Junior School, Ealing

This Is Me!

I like science, astronomy too,
I know the name of many planets, but exoplanets only a few,
I like cosmology, the planets and stars,
And I know many facts, especially about Mars!
I like to learn from websites and books,
And fact files about NASA is where I really like to look!
I spend my time reading in the morning and at night,
And if someone disturbs me, don't worry, I won't bite!
I have many books on the mysteries of the universe,
But if you asked me to perform in a play, I wouldn't know one verse!
This is me, I am who I'm meant to be!

Saina Bhatia (10)
Notting Hill & Ealing Junior School, Ealing

What Is My Favourite Food?

My favourite food, my favourite food,
It's long like the spaghetti in bolognese,
And it puts me in a happy mood,
It also makes me have a certain craze,

It originates in Asia, the biggest continent of them all,
And can by eaten with chopsticks,
They are scrumptious, long and tall,
It's my favourite food out of anything I could pick,

My favourite food, my favourite food,
To know the correct answer will put your brain to the test,
It puts me in a happy mood,
Come and take a guess?

Answer: Chinese noodles.

Violet Muralidhar (10)
Notting Hill & Ealing Junior School, Ealing

Facts

Facts, wonderful things to describe me
Say I eat cucumber every day
Or that 'Totally' and
'Why not?' are my favourite words to say

One, I never use a knife and fork
Two, 'tis not often that I lie
Three, Big Nate is my favourite book
Four, I rarely ever cry

I'm quite talented because
Only at the age of two
(In Chinese, for a fact,)
I made a poem about poos!

See what I mean?
A great way to introduce
(Bonus fact
My favourite word is 'abstruse').

Violetta Cheng (8)
Notting Hill & Ealing Junior School, Ealing

Thoughts About Me!

D aring! I try out new ideas
I nspiring! I try to be and creative with new thoughts
Y outhful! I love to play
A dventurous! I try taking risks

D ogs! Oh, my favourite one
I mpalas! Oh, the patterned horns
Y aks! Oh, so big and strong
A rctic foxes! Oh, so fluffy and white

D rawing! Always a favourite past time
I nterpretation! From Reads, always a challenge
Y earn! Always a puppy
A wesome! Always wanna be...

Diya Nayak (10)
Notting Hill & Ealing Junior School, Ealing

This Is Me

My own appearance
Might be my family's influence, but I will always have
My own difference

My own hereditary
Will make a large part of
My own identity

My own ambition
Whether a bright mathematician or performance musician, it's
My own decision

My own values
Which I shall choose, will be based on
My own views

My own thoughts
That no one can force are from
My own source

My own destiny
What will be will be
This is *me!*

Aline Topalian (8)
Notting Hill & Ealing Junior School, Ealing

This Is Me

I don't like vegetables or fruit,
But I love netball and I love to shoot.
I am really interested in planets and stars,
I like eating all chocolate from Galaxy to Mars.

I am creative and enjoy art,
I love to act and play the part.
One of my hobbies is writing a book,
I don't like to bake or to cook.

People would describe me as chatty and funny,
My hair is blonde, the colour of honey.
Guitar is the instrument I like to play,
And if I could, I would skateboard all day.

Ottilie Calvert (9)
Notting Hill & Ealing Junior School, Ealing

Amazing Me

This is me!
Am I right or left-handed?
Stay healthy all the time!
Getting really jolly!
I hope you'll never mind,
Eating great food!
I hope the puddings never lie!
Getting really grumpy when you're learning about time,
Looking in the dictionary when there are tricky words to find!
Maybe helping to make dinner!
I hope it's really yummy too!
Dreaming about the future!
Your brains are always full of stuff,
Wake up in the morning,
With a big smile on your dial!

Hannah Clough (7)
Notting Hill & Ealing Junior School, Ealing

Me And Zebras

A gatha is amazing
G ood at many things
A rt and astronomy
T hese are all her favourite things
H aving to write poems
A lways makes her grumpy

C limbing walls and sliding down ropes
H oping that she won't fall off
A s she tries to win a race
R unning at top speed
E very metre getting harder as she
M errily passes the finish line
Z ebras don't like poetry
A nd neither do I.

Agatha Charemza-Caunt (9)
Notting Hill & Ealing Junior School, Ealing

If I Am Not I Would Be

If I'm not a lion, I'm a tiger,
If I'm not a tiger, I'm a cheetah,
If I'm not a cheetah, I'm a leopard,
If I'm not a leopard, I'm something,
I'm a special, unique and awesome something,
And I try to let my inner self shine through,
I also worry too,
I worry about a million things,
That aren't even going to come true,
It's a superpower really, a work of art,
Though I really can't control my heart,
I have to choose to be a brave lion.

Poppy Roberts (9)
Notting Hill & Ealing Junior School, Ealing

My Journey

My journey was tough, dancing was really rough.
I dance my heart out and move all about.
When I see people perform, it makes me warm.
One day, I'd like to meet other artists because I'm the smartest.
If I could choose my job, I'd be a dancer and that's my answer, *boom!*
As I drink my tea, I see a part of me
Dancing in the moonlight sky as I fly high!
As I dream, I think of a meme of me dancing,
And that's the end of my rhyme,
Yours next time.

Jessie Kolawole (8)
Notting Hill & Ealing Junior School, Ealing

This Is My Poem

My name is Isabella,
My daddy calls me Rockafella, Terror, Umbrella,
But he never mentions it to "Abuela".
I have two kittens, they are so cute,
But they always go mute.
I go to ballet on Saturdays,
I say to my daddy, "Come along," but he says, "No way, Jose."
I always play with my friends, I call them mates.
On play dates, I hand out cakes on plates.
'Woo-woos' are my favourite drinks,
Because they are the colour pink!

Isabella Eleanor Hayes (8)
Notting Hill & Ealing Junior School, Ealing

Reading Is Life

I am a book lover,

Last term I read cover after cover,
On my bed.
Vacation? Nope, reading instead,
Every day I think of something new.

Reading instead of eating stew,
Even when it's time for school.
Always writing, not swimming in the pool.
Dreadful when it's time for bed,
I could be reading instead.
Now I have to stop,
Going to eat from the pot.

Rhea Franklin (8)
Notting Hill & Ealing Junior School, Ealing

Reading

Reading is like air to me
I can't live without the books I read
When I read, I get lost in make-believe lands
The forest, Green Gables, Elizabethan times, fairy-tale worlds
It's my favourite thing to do
Nothing is better than settling down with a book
And reading
When people call my name
Whilst I'm in the forest
It seems so far off that I just ignore them
I feel like I'm a different person
And it's another me they're calling.

Sahi Shah (9)
Notting Hill & Ealing Junior School, Ealing

Magnificent Me

A lways loves to read books
M aking cakes that look so good
E very day makes me extremely happy
Y ear Four girls are very yappy
A pples are my favourite fruit

B ecause they give you such a shoot
A mazing Harry takes a rest
R on and Hermione come second best
K elloggs Crunchy Nut is sweet
E ating it is such a treat
R unning round the huge court, netball is my
favourite sport.

Ameya Barker (8)
Notting Hill & Ealing Junior School, Ealing

This Is Me!

My hair is blonde
I love to sing
My life is full of musical things.
My family is great
My friends are kind
I love to do yoga
To help me unwind.
On Saturday mornings
To Questors I go
Acting and drama
Is how I like to flow.
The planet and animals
Are close to my heart
By being a vegetarian
Is how I play my eco-part
Like a Duracell bunny
I can keep going all day
When I have a goal
Nothing stands in my way!

Camille Sanderson (7)
Notting Hill & Ealing Junior School, Ealing

Charlotte Groocock

Charlotte, that's me
I like drinking tea
People think I'm funny
I like toast and honey
I play the guitar
I'd like to be a star
I love food to munch
Especially at lunch
QPR is the best team
As you can see, I am very keen
Lego is one of my favourite things
I like to eat baked beans from a tin
I'm a stubborn little fellow
And my favourite colour is yellow
I like chicken pie and that's really not a lie.

Charlotte Groocock (8)
Notting Hill & Ealing Junior School, Ealing

My Favourite Item

His long arms are perfect for cuddling,
They keep me warm and toasty like a s'more,
A giant smile shines on his face,
Can you guess who it is?
It can do forward rolls better than me!
My favourite item is him.

We have been on many great adventures across the seven seas!
I know that he is always up to jumping in a puddle.
I love this item,
It is my favourite item of them all!
Not guessed yet?
It is my teddy, Big Sloth!

Cara Morrissey (10)
Notting Hill & Ealing Junior School, Ealing

What I Love

I love ducks so much,
Their cute little faces,
Crunch go their teeth, *crunch, crunch,*
They are in all types of places,
I love stories about a chick's nest,
Sometimes it's a bit of a quest,
I read and read so much sometimes,
During the daytime and night-time,
I read while I do cartwheels,
I can't do it at school, sad,
I can squeal,
I go crazy mad,
My favourite food is dim sum,
This is me.

Eila Shah (9)
Notting Hill & Ealing Junior School, Ealing

Magnificent Me

J ust a cheeky monkey who's going to go far.
A n Indian girl who wants to be a movie star.
S he loves to sing herself to sleep instead of counting silly sheep.
M agnificent she is and so proud to be a Sikh.
I f dancing was ever banned, she would have a big frown.
N ot that that would ever happen in this tremendous town.
E ventually this poem must come to an end, but still she hopes to be your best friend.

Jasmine Takhar (7)
Notting Hill & Ealing Junior School, Ealing

If I Were A Toy

You sit on me, towering over everyone,
Brave and courageous,
You love me, feed me and braid my hair.

I am your family, I stay by your side,
Loyal and unbreakable,
You care for me, play with me and stroke me.

I can be as fast as a cheetah, as slow as a tortoise,
Dappled and grey,
I am unique, different and special.

I rock to and fro, I go high and low,
What am I?

Answer: A rocking horse.

Isabel Saunders (8)
Notting Hill & Ealing Junior School, Ealing

This Is Me

I love to read, I love to draw,
But I love my family even more,
Sometimes I'm a drama queen,
Running around like a crazy machine,
Everyone who knows me will agree...
This is me!
I'm very brave,
I might *sometimes* misbehave...
I'm generous, I'm funny,
I love bread dipped in honey,
I'm fast and speedy,
I don't like food too creamy,
Everyone who knows me will agree...
This is me!

Sophie Tan (10)
Notting Hill & Ealing Junior School, Ealing

About Amazing Amari

Amari is my name
I'm different, not the same
Caring and kind
With a hard-working mind
I like things tidy and clean
Helping Mummy use Mr Sheen
I can swim very fast
Don't want to come last
My sister and I like to play
She's cheeky and she always gets her way
I have a delightful smile
And legs as long as the river Nile
Family is what's important, you see
It keeps on growing just like me.

Amari Nanda (9)
Notting Hill & Ealing Junior School, Ealing

This Is Me

T hough I am skinny, bony with chicken legs
H ow I love chocolate, fries and scrambled eggs
I greatly enjoy cooking with my mummy
S ometimes what we create is just so yummy

I can be clumsy, fidgety and sometimes with two left feet
S omehow I turn super sporty when I compete

M y friends find me amusing and awfully funny
E specially when I dance like a gangster granny.

Bella Brathwaite (9)
Notting Hill & Ealing Junior School, Ealing

I Love Living My Life

I love ballet and netball when it's sunny.
I love music, especially if I choose it.
If my love of books crawled out of me,
It would borrow all the books in the library.
I would love to have a pet,
Then my childhood goals would be met.
I love attending my local church and singing
Amazing Grace.
I love being with my family and friends
They make me feel special.
I love playing my violin because it keeps me
smiling.

Wala Chellah (9)

Notting Hill & Ealing Junior School, Ealing

Deep, Deep Inside

I am mischievous, brave and kind.
I am a bouncing bunny and a curious hunter.
My love is strong deep, deep inside
and will one day tear through the villages, valleys, lakes and rivers.
My joy reflects back to you and me
like doves drifting through the air.
No matter where you and I are
we are always together and there is freedom in my kingdom.
We are a family united and together
with a pinch of magic, can solve all.

Emily Angela Craven (10)
Notting Hill & Ealing Junior School, Ealing

My Dream

I want to be an artist, I want to be an engineer
D reams can go anywhere, I hope they don't disappear
E ngineers are cool with all the designing, testing and inspecting
A rtists are creative, your ideas can go wild.

G o for it, I'll give it my all
O pportunities to want
A dventures to explore
L ook forward to my goals
S miling all the way like the sun.

Karina Patel (8)
Notting Hill & Ealing Junior School, Ealing

Risk-Taking Me!

R isk-taking me.
I love to be as wild as a lion.
S tarting when I was very young.
K icking balls is my fun.

T ime passed.
A nd I am still wild and now
K icking and jumping like a dancer
I s me!
N ever afraid to take a risk
G ood-natured like a fish

M eerkats are my favourite animals
E verything said, it's me!

Zoe Pole (8)
Notting Hill & Ealing Junior School, Ealing

I Am Theodora

I have rosy cheeks and a big smile,
Brown hair and a fancy style.
I love dreaming big dreams,
I like pasta and ice creams.
I have a great big family tree,
I love them and they love me.
I am fond of animals, especially cats,
Leopards, dogs and upside-down bats.
I love dancing, reading and having fun,
And I like to play in the sun.
I enjoy splashing in the sea,
These are the things that make me, me.

Theodora Liakou (8)
Notting Hill & Ealing Junior School, Ealing

Reading

R eading is the best as it lets out all the stress!
E veryone can read a book when feeling quite depressed
A witch, now a wizard, now a fairy in the next book
D etails that will make you feel just so hooked
I n-between the chapters, snuck downstairs for a snack
N othing's gonna stop you from coming straight back
G o on! Give reading a try - it's a favourite hobby of mine.

Ella Mistry (9)

Notting Hill & Ealing Junior School, Ealing

My Hair!

Plaits standing to attention,
Fishtails, braids, bunches, ponytails swishing
through the air.
These are all found in my hair.

It's thick, brown, long just like a horse's mane.
Sometimes smooth, sometimes knotty, brushing is
a pain!

Fragrant after a bubblebath,
Haribo scented shampoo would make me laugh!

Sometimes I like to chew my hair
It gets a bit soggy but I don't care!

Amaya Roy-Bird (8)
Notting Hill & Ealing Junior School, Ealing

How To Make Millie

Make sure you have a recipe book.
Make sure you have a bowl.
According to your recipe, you need to add
A sprinkle of stardust.
Add a pinch of awesomeness.
Add a drop of pretty.
Mix the batter.
While mixing, add a drop of kindness, being caring
And cleverness.
Continue to mix.
Pour batter in a body shape mould.
Bake for seven and three-quarter hours.
There you have it, your own Millie.

Millie Lockett-Boyle (7)
Notting Hill & Ealing Junior School, Ealing

What Makes Me, Me!

L is for lively, that is my personality
A is for angel in my mum's eye
R is for radiant, humble and kind
A is for admirable, my daddy's pride

S is for spring, the season I was born
H is for helpful, that's my nature
E is for elegance that I exude
T is for thoughtful, always considerate
H is for honest, full of integrity.

Lara Sheth (7)
Notting Hill & Ealing Junior School, Ealing

This Is Me

This is me
I like trees
I don't like peas
And I like bees
I like unicorns
Pegasi and alicorns
And I definitely like
Some yummy sweetcorn
I have a mango coloured fountain pen
And by the way, did you know that I'm ten?
I would never say no to some ice cream, as long as it has whipped cream
This is me
I like the breeze
And I like palm trees
And I might like cheese.

Iyla Sridharan (10)
Notting Hill & Ealing Junior School, Ealing

This Is Me

My favourite things are sport and art,
They never fail to fill my heart,
In cricket, I have learnt some tricks,
And with my bat, I can hit a six,
Colours of the rainbow and colours of the sea,
And colours of the world are dear to me,
But most of all, I like to spend,
Time with my dear friends,
My family is the best thing I could ever wish for,
Nothing would please me more.
This is me!

Neena Chowdhry-Qureshi (7)
Notting Hill & Ealing Junior School, Ealing

Hanna Wahid

H umble heart of happiness
A s graceful as a swan
N imble, agile and full of energy
N etball is my favourite sport
A lthough I love gymnastics too.

W itty and bright, I'm like a flower blooming
A mbitious and resilient I am
H afsa is my sister whilst
I sa is my brother
D edicated, dynamic and determined, this is me!

Hanna Wahid (10)
Notting Hill & Ealing Junior School, Ealing

I Wish I Was A Wizard

I wish I was a wizard
I would know lots of spells and potions
So I could fly myself to school or
Make myself lucky in an exam

I wish I was a wizard
Then I could protect the people I love
May my family never get sick
And my friends never get harmed

I wish I was a wizard
So I could change the world
By giving each person a love potion
Bringing peace across oceans.

Emily Lau (8)
Notting Hill & Ealing Junior School, Ealing

My Name

Hi, I'm Esme,
But you can call me Emse,
Or Smesme,
Or Smosme,
Or maybe just Osme,
How about Smezzles?
Perhaps Ezzle-Wezzles,
Possibly Smozzles,
Do you think Ozze-Wozzles?
Now, these are all options,
But there's another choice,
And honestly, truthfully,
It's really rather nice,
Wait just a second,
One... Two... Three...
How about...
Me!

Esme Gowlland (11)
Notting Hill & Ealing Junior School, Ealing

This Is Me

T here is usually a warm smile on my face.
H appy to be with my family and friends.
I will try to persevere and develop my talents.
S illy fun with my friends always makes me laugh.

I will try to be kind and considerate,
S o I can be proud of what I am.

M e being true to myself is what matters.
E xcited for what my future holds.

Eshwari Maruthainar (8)
Notting Hill & Ealing Junior School, Ealing

Savannah

S illy sometimes when I do my banana dance!
A wesome! when I'm doing the splits.
V ivacious in my personality.
A mazing no matter what.
N imble, especially when I'm running!
N atural in being who I am.
A mbitious when I'm always aiming high.
H umorous when I say silly jokes.

M e - there is no one more me than me!

Savannah McDowell (7)
Notting Hill & Ealing Junior School, Ealing

This Is Me

Bookworm, always got my nose across the page,
And music in my head as I move across the dance floor,
Adventures from head to toe,

Cartwheeling across the piano,
Chatting note to note,
Sometimes a quaver, sometimes a crotchet or a semitone,

Loud I can be when I read,
My mind moving quickly,
As quiet as a mouse, my eyes wide,
Watching a movie,

This is me!

Amelie Moses (9)
Notting Hill & Ealing Junior School, Ealing

My Life

This is me
Energy thriving
Gaming is my thing
Can't wait to get swimming.
My friends say I'm chatty
My mum says I'm fidgety
Got a sister, she's annoying
I have a brother to add to that.
I hate grammar, it's the worst
Punctuation is no better, of course.
Let's have a disco, BFFs,
Now you know me better than ever
We will party all day long.

Caitlin Fratter (9)
Notting Hill & Ealing Junior School, Ealing

How To Be Me

T o be me, you must be lots of fun,
H elpful, kind and considerate,
I am hardworking but still courageous,
S o must you be if you want to be me.

I am adventurous, persevering but calm,
S till keeping up with all of my traits.

M aybe you are like me, full of laughter,
E ven if you are, you will still never be the true me.

Erin Sanderson (10)
Notting Hill & Ealing Junior School, Ealing

All About My Clevernesses

I am as sharp as a dart,
I have a big heart

My parents say to be proud,
But sometimes I can be loud

In a deep dark forest, I like to forage,
This shows I have courage

I enjoy honey,
And I can be funny

I can be fun,
But I don't like playing with a gun

Everyone thinks tigers are deadly,
Just like me, I think they are friendly.

Laranya Ryatt (7)
Notting Hill & Ealing Junior School, Ealing

Special Me

Everyone says I am very kind,
They also say I have a beautiful mind.
My mother says I am a star,
And I will go very, very far.
I shine bright like a sun,
I am also a lot of fun,
I make my parents very proud,
Though sometimes I can be loud,
I always try to be good.
I like to have a good mood,
I am not too tall,
Yet not too small,
I try to be the best of all.

Sophia Almanov (7)
Notting Hill & Ealing Junior School, Ealing

Me!

C hloe is a loving girl
H er favourite colour is green
L oyal, friendly, full of beans
O ptimistic but never mean
E very day she tries her best

A nd loves with all her heart
L aughter's like heaven to her and
L earning makes her feel smart
E ven if her day isn't great
N ever will she fall apart.

Chloe Allen (8)
Notting Hill & Ealing Junior School, Ealing

Friends

F riends are God's greatest gift
R are like double rainbows radiating in the sky
I nseparable like a beautiful bond between
identical twins
E ndearing like a beautiful baby's beam
N oblest relationship in the whole wide world
D ark clouds of tears replaced by sunlit, summery
sky
S ilver lining in your sorrows, sadness and low
spirits.

Aadhya Parikh (8)
Notting Hill & Ealing Junior School, Ealing

Colourful Decision

I am colourful and just to your liking,
You can adjust me in any way.
Start again, or do another,
That is your choice!
I do not make any noise,
In fact, I cannot,
But you can spoil me with dots.
And lots and lots of spots,
I can be anything,
In or out,
Up or down.
You use pencils to shape me!
And crayons to make me!
What am I?
I am a drawing!

Kate Mak (9)
Notting Hill & Ealing Junior School, Ealing

Ballet

B allet lets me express my emotions... Buckets of joy rush through my veins.
A mbitiously, I want to succeed in being the most exquisite and elegant dancer.
L ovingly and beautifully I sway, reaching for the sparkling stars.
L avishly graceful, I point my light toes.
E ven though at times it can be tough, I am determined to keep on going.
T his is me!

Mehar Kaur Sekhon (9)
Notting Hill & Ealing Junior School, Ealing

Amazing Me

L ovely Lara is who I am,
A nimal lover - big and small,
R eally artistic, painting pretty pictures,
A mazing, friendly and funny too,

H elping family around the house,
I ntelligent, busy bookworm
C aring, cheerful and also creative,
K ind like a brownie should be,
S trong and smart - that's me!

Lara Hicks (8)
Notting Hill & Ealing Junior School, Ealing

Lyla Peat

L oving is what I am
Y ouTube is what I love to watch
L aughing is what I can't control
A nimals are something I love

P hoebe, my younger sister, would always play with me
E mpire Family is what I watch on YouTube
A n actress is what I would love to be
T easing my sister is what I sometimes do.

Lyla Peat (8)
Notting Hill & Ealing Junior School, Ealing

Me

This is me,
Sitting, reading in the corner of my room, getting sucked into another good book.
This is me,
Sprinting up and down the netball court with my team ready to win.
This is me,
Heart thumping, waiting for the horn to go so I can launch myself into the water.
This is me,
Staring out the window, drifting away from the world, lost in my thoughts.

Alice Wilson-Brown (9)
Notting Hill & Ealing Junior School, Ealing

All About Me

H ettie is what I get called
E very day.
N obody calls me Henrietta.
R eally I just want my own room but
I have to share with my sister for the moment.
E nglish is my favourite subject.
T hough I want to be better at maths.
T omorrow I have a swimming gala.
A nd that is me.

Hettie Heppenstall (7)
Notting Hill & Ealing Junior School, Ealing

All About Me

My name is Juno and I like to play Uno.
My favourite bird is a dove and I like the word 'love'.
My favourite season is summer and homework is such a bummer.
When I eat chocolate, I go, "Yum, yum, yum. Where did you get this, Mum?"
I especially like Lindor. What more?
I normally fancy sweet treats. I'm big with daydreams.

Juno Psaropoulou (7)
Notting Hill & Ealing Junior School, Ealing

I Am Me!

G rateful for help and gifts.
E nergetic and full of enthusiasm.
O ptimistic for lots of things. It is
R ight that I sometimes get frustrated. I normally am feeling
G reat!
I f I get angry, I calm down quite fast.
A nd I am usually happy. When you put those together...

I am me!

Georgia Shebbeare (7)
Notting Hill & Ealing Junior School, Ealing

I Am Kind

I like to make people happy,

A nd I feel sad when others feel bad,
M y friends and my sister sometimes cry,

K indness is a key that I can always try,
I t unlocks joy in others' hearts,
N ow I know this, I feel smart,
D oing everything I can for others is where I start!

Florence Bonner (7)
Notting Hill & Ealing Junior School, Ealing

This Is Me!

A bucketful of courage to meet the world's challenges.
A never-ending stream of love to care for friends and family.
A pinch of anxiety because no one is perfect.
Ten truckloads of happiness because I am as bright as the sun.
A few bottles of smiles and laughs to make the world a wonderful place.

This is me!

Surya Chauhan (9)
Notting Hill & Ealing Junior School, Ealing

Who Is Sienna?

S porty Sienna plays cricket, netball and tennis
I nquisitive Sienna always asks how and why
E nergetic Sienna adores dancing to upbeat music
N ice Sienna shares her chocolate
N aughty Sienna conveniently forgets to make her bed
A dventurous Sienna enjoys climbing trees like a koala.

Sienna Patel (8)
Notting Hill & Ealing Junior School, Ealing

Who Am I?

Who am I,
Who am I?
I'll give you some clues,
But first I need to tell you
My favourite colour's blue,
I live in Kingshill with a toy or two,
I bet you didn't know
But my favourite animals are koalas,
I bet your thoughts are different
But my message for today is
We are all unique.

Summer Zhang (7)
Notting Hill & Ealing Junior School, Ealing

What Makes Me

I am happiness, I'm joy,
I am smart, I am kind, I am creative,
I am risk-taking, I am helpful,
I am laughing, I am giggling,
This is what makes me!

I am swimming, I am dancing,
I am Minecraft, I am Roblox,
I am the Switch, I am Mario,
I am fashion, I am lucky,
This is what makes me!

Eliza O'Connell (7)
Notting Hill & Ealing Junior School, Ealing

This Is Me

M y nickname at home
O therwise known as Esme
N ever seen with straight hair
K eeps my room awesomely tidy and
L oves making everyone's beds!
E xcited by swimming in glistening pools, cold
lochs and turquoise seas
S wims like a fish; watch me at the gala and see!

Esme Whiteman (7)
Notting Hill & Ealing Junior School, Ealing

This Is Me

This is me
Tall and cool
Energetic and fun
My nemesis is maths
I can barely sit still
Practise netball in the garden
Gaming is my jam
Put on some music
Get in the pool
Can't wait to do front crawl
Chatting with my besties
Never remember
My capital letters
This is me.

Leonora Clarke (10)
Notting Hill & Ealing Junior School, Ealing

All About Me

E xcellent person.
M ature child.
M ummy's girl.
A lexander's sister.

L oves macaroons.
O utdoors type.
U nderstanding person.
I like Lego like my dad.
S neaky girl.
E njoys spending time with friends and family.

Emma Louise Melikian (8)
Notting Hill & Ealing Junior School, Ealing

This Is Me

I am bravery
I am bone
I will not crack, nor break, nor shatter
But sometimes I need to be left alone.

I am sporty, kind and funny
Popular is me too
I love being friendly
What about you?

I know that I
Can do anything
The time flies by
While I sing.

Swara Dusad (8)
Notting Hill & Ealing Junior School, Ealing

Me!

L ike a spider spins its web
I 'll spin a fairy tale
L ike the hummingbird beats its wings
I 'll race my fingers across the piano keys
A s the sun shines true and bright
N ew wonders are the things I seek
A ray of sunshine is what I am.

Liliana Razlog (9)
Notting Hill & Ealing Junior School, Ealing

I Am Dheeksha

D aring enough to accept a challenge
H onest and trustworthy friend
E xciting person to be with
E njoys playing with cats
K een on learning badminton
S inging songs all the time
H arry Potter is my favourite book
A dmires history.

Dheeksha Mani (8)
Notting Hill & Ealing Junior School, Ealing

What Quality Am I?

A riddle

My force is like a spring in perpetual motion.
I am as fast as a cheetah chasing chimps.
My step is as lively as a bouncy, boisterous balloon.
I race and don't stop like a Lamborghini with limitless fuel.

What quality am I?

Answer: Energetic.

Anna Oxley-Tran (8)
Notting Hill & Ealing Junior School, Ealing

This Is Me!

T his is me
H appy doing gymnastics
I play with my friends a lot
S mall procrastinator

I love swimming and diving
S hy sometimes

M e and my family are inseparable
E xcitable at times.

Kassie Hamill (9)
Notting Hill & Ealing Junior School, Ealing

Swimming

S uper fast, gliding through the water.
W e practise racing everywhere.
I love swimming.
M y body moving gracefully.
M y mind focused.
I tumble turn in the water.
N ever giving up.
G oing for gold.

Eleanor Sculthorpe (8)
Notting Hill & Ealing Junior School, Ealing

I Am Maggie

M y friends make me giggle like a monkey.
A lways smiling around people.
G oing swimming makes my heart race.
G ames with family are fun.
I feel awesome when I do well.
E xcitement grows when I try something new.

Maggie Wilson-Brown (7)
Notting Hill & Ealing Junior School, Ealing

This Is Who I Am

E verything is energetic,
L azy times too,
L aughing and dancing,
A lways a challenge.

Who am I, happy or sad?
What am I, human or fish?
When am I? Usually late!
Why am I?

I am going to find out!

Ella Swift (11)
Notting Hill & Ealing Junior School, Ealing

Me

I like to eat,
Especially meat.

Birds have beaks,
I can do leaps.

I like to dance,
And I like to glance.

I like swimming,
And giggling.

Even though I am a child,
I can run ten miles.

Yvie Huang (8)
Notting Hill & Ealing Junior School, Ealing

Isobel

I ntelligent with my school work.
S ensible most of the time.
O riginal, there's no one like me.
B eautiful inside and out.
E xcellent at being kind.
L oving to everyone around me.

Isobel MacDougall (7)
Notting Hill & Ealing Junior School, Ealing

My Fantastic Life!

Hello, my name is Tamara
My head a pool of thoughts
As I gaze at the stars
With my telescope
Viewing the sky so high
I dream of other worlds
Swimming deep in my thoughts
Towards my bright future.

Tamara Kanesamuttunathan (8)
Notting Hill & Ealing Junior School, Ealing

A Description Of Me!

A kennings poem

I am a...

Friend maker,
Fun lover,
Secret sharer,
Hard worker,
Late riser,
Ice cream licker,
Chocolate eater,
Messy writer,
Accompanier,
And finally...
A great friend!

Ira Trivedi (9)
Notting Hill & Ealing Junior School, Ealing

This Is Me

A kennings poem

Story reader
Lego builder
Deep sleeper
Bucket filler
Fast speaker
Sometimes untidy
Chocolate eater
Always lively
Usually sympathetic
Reliably friendly
Intermittently energetic.

Georgie Grecos (8)
Notting Hill & Ealing Junior School, Ealing

Maths

M aths is my strength.
A mazing things I do in maths.
T errific speed I do maths in.
"H ow can you do that?" people sometimes ask me.
S uper as a star I am at maths.

Millie Milne (7)

Notting Hill & Ealing Junior School, Ealing

A Young Lioness

H umble Hafsa who loves baking.
A mazing artist in the making.
F antastic friend who's always there.
S uper sister who loves to care.
A young lioness is her namesake.

Hafsa Wahid (8)
Notting Hill & Ealing Junior School, Ealing

This Is Me!

M agical like dazzling, booming fireworks.
A mazing like a spectacular shooting star.
Y outhful like the first beautiful spring flowers.
A dventurous like a soaring mighty albatross.

Maya Richardson (7)
Notting Hill & Ealing Junior School, Ealing

This Is Me

A kennings poem

Kind carer
Sarcastic sayer
Relative lover
Friend maker
Funny talker
Forgetful leaver
People annoyer
Artistic painter
Messy eater
Room untidier
Super swimmer.

Lilly Murphy (9)
Notting Hill & Ealing Junior School, Ealing

Happy

H appiness is the best emotion
A smile is what you need
P lus laughs and kindness
P ure friends are great
Y ou should be happy!

Nikita Pillai (8)
Notting Hill & Ealing Junior School, Ealing

I Am...

A kennings poem

I am a...
Book reader
Chocolate eater
Animal lover
Bold actor
Puzzle craver
Planet saver
Bug fleer
Great helper

This is me.

Shreya Thakar (9)
Notting Hill & Ealing Junior School, Ealing

Tilly

A kennings poem

Art maker
Saucepan shaker
Tennis player
Bun baker
Canvas painter
Jenga builder
Early waker
Woodland explorer
Animal adorer.

Tilly Neslen (9)
Notting Hill & Ealing Junior School, Ealing

Me!

A kennings poem

Problem solver
Mischief maker
Book reader
Kindness sharer
Friends maker
Science tester
Happiness giver
Sewing superstar.

Amaya Syan (9)
Notting Hill & Ealing Junior School, Ealing

Who Am I?

I am a pony lover
A dramatic actor
A strong swimmer
A master chef
And an artistic artist
Who am I?

Sophie Taylor.

Sophie Taylor (10)
Notting Hill & Ealing Junior School, Ealing

I'm Just A Girl

My name is Louisse, I like to eat cheese.
I'm really good at maths but not at paths.
I love all my writing, yet I don't like fighting.
When I play all my instruments, I get all the compliments.
I walk to school and I try to be cool.
I study really hard to get a great report card.
I'm working for a pen license and I'm kind of good at science.
I know my times tables and I'm learning basketball,
I think that's all, but one more thing, I'm not that tall.

Louisse-Margarette Nepomuceno (8)
Sacred Heart RC Primary School, Battersea

My Beautiful Life

S ophia is my name.
O range is my favourite colour.
P oems are amazing.
H istory is my thing.
I ce cream is my favourite sweet.
A nia is my lovely mum.

S ummer is my favourite season.
A ryan is my fun brother.
G randma bakes the best cakes.
G ymnastics make me so excited.
A pples are juicy fruits.
R eading makes me smart.

Sophia Saggar (7)
Sacred Heart RC Primary School, Battersea

This Is Me

My name is Beau
Here's a little something you should know
I have a sister called Sky who acts very shy
And a sister called Faith who makes me feel safe
I've got a mum and dad
Who makes me feel happy when I am sad
Thank you for your time and listening to my rhyme
Let me end here
And enjoy the rest of your year.

Beau Exton (8)
Sacred Heart RC Primary School, Battersea

Fun Things To Do

I looked at the light and it felt like I was shining bright
For a while, I was flying a kite
Suddenly, it was as hot as a cooking pot.
Then, I went to the pet shop
To get the pet that I wanted to name.
So I went to go make a home
I went and it was a fake nest.
Soon, it was night-time and I was fine
So I went to sleep.

Samuel Aka (8)
Sacred Heart RC Primary School, Battersea

Humble Boy

I am a dark-skinned boy with bright, sparkling eyes.
With sharp, listening ears like that of a lion.
Kind-hearted and helpful to all,
Not many like me yet I'm humble as always.
I am the charm of all and so shall I be
Attentive in class and a great role model.
I ask God to help me be as I am
Now and forever.

Jaiden-Ryan Ampah (8)
Sacred Heart RC Primary School, Battersea

What Colour?

Is it blue, pink or red?
There is a lot more that isn't said.

Pink and green,
Oh no; can never be seen.

Maybe pink,
Let's check the link.

Brown, let me think,
On second thought, it makes me sick.

What colour?
I know...
Rainbow.

Otega Dinham-Atakpo (7)
Sacred Heart RC Primary School, Battersea

This Is Me

I'm Panos, a young boy,
Full of love and full of joy.
I worry, I cry,
I fight, I try.
I'm blue, I'm yellow,
I'm a rainbow fellow.
I travel, I stay,
I dream, I pray.
For now, I'm fine,
But one day I will shine.

Panos-Ektoras Christou (7)

Sacred Heart RC Primary School, Battersea

Amazing Me!

I wear glasses, play the piano
When I'm bored, I get ready for art.
Which colour - blue, red, green, purple or all of them?
I do art, piano, games and do my homework!
The recipe for me is art, piano, glasses, running and kindness.

Dylan Moran (8)
Sacred Heart RC Primary School, Battersea

This Is Me

T his is my poem.
H appy, loving friends caring for one another.
I sometimes help people when they all fall, and when I fall over, they all come over to help.
S inging while reading all my books with my funny friends all day long.

I love hanging out with my friends.
S chool is my favourite, especially the teacher, all my friends and maths.

M aking people laugh by making books all the time.
E specially I love my family.

This is me.

Jack (8)
Western Primary School, Grimsby

This Is Me!

T he best part about school is learning.
H appy, I have the best class and family.
I am smart and love to read books.
S inging and dancing are my dream.

I have eyes as green as an emerald and hair as long as Rapunzel.
S ometimes I put on make-up as soft as a baby bear's fur.

M y future is being a mummy because I love my mum.
E ating is my favourite thing, but school is even better!

Winnie (7)

Western Primary School, Grimsby

This Is Me!

I can fly like a bird on the swings at the park.
I am as happy as the sun shining at me.
I am as smart as a scientist doing an experiment.
I am as sweet as a nurse helping a patient.
I am as cheeky as a monkey taking sweets before bed.
I am as big as a mum monkey.
My hair is as dark as brown chocolate.
I am scared of losing my baby cousin Daisy because she is so little.
I am as brave as a bear in danger.

This is me!

Hattie (7)
Western Primary School, Grimsby

This Is Me

T he girl who loves school.
H air as tasty-looking as chocolate.
I love learning maths.
S easide is my favourite place in the world.

I am happy when I play with my sister.
S ometimes I play with her on the bouncy blue trampoline.

M e and my sister play games, my favourite game is hide-and-seek.
E lephants are my favourite animal because they've got flappy ears.

Olivia Woods (8)
Western Primary School, Grimsby

This Is Me

As quick as a tap
As slow as a turtle
As sticky as a glue stick

As soft as a bottle of shampoo
As short as a giraffe
As tall as a baby
As quiet as a glass smashing
As loud as a lady dropping from the sky
As sharp as a book
As smooth as a pencil tip
As twisted as a ruler

As straight as paper
As fancy as a fascinated man

As boring as a clown
As lazy as Mrs Mumby.

Lexi-Mae Wilkinson (9)
Western Primary School, Grimsby

Megan, This Is Me!

This is me!
I am as kind as a teacher.
I am as curious as a cat.
I am as sweet as sugar.
I am as cheeky as a monkey throwing poo!
I am an art maker.
I am a pretty flower.
I am a music listener.
I am a scrunchie wearer.
I am a lizard lover.
I am a game player after school.
I am a chatty parrot.
My hair is a bar of chocolate.
I smile in the sun while eating ice cream!
This is me!

Megan Buston (8)
Western Primary School, Grimsby

This Is Me... Destiny

T his is me!
H appy as a monkey throwing a banana.
I love swimming underwater with my sisters.
S ometimes I play with my playful dog Domino.

I love school and learning and I love my teachers,
they are kind and caring.
S ometimes I stay with the teacher at dinner.

M y three sisters annoy me every day.
E very day, my sisters are sat on their phones.

Destiny Baker-Tinmurth (8)
Western Primary School, Grimsby

This Is Me

As fast as a snail
As scary as Mrs Mumby
As bright as the night

As funny as a clown
As brave as a lion

As brave as a cucumber

As high as the sky
As busy as a bee
As lazy as a tree

As slow as a cheetah
As kind as a monkey
As feral as a frog

As pretty as the sea

As short as a worm
As mean as a butterfly
As boring as the finish.

Kyla (9)
Western Primary School, Grimsby

This Is Me

T iny as a ladybird
H appy as a monkey
I love dogs and puppies
S miling like my cheeky, greedy dog when he eats my chocolate

I like to chase my dog around like a cat
S ix children who annoy me every day although Freddie, Archie and Harley are the worst

M y brothers are on their phones all day
E lephant ears that are as big as a human!

Lester (8)
Western Primary School, Grimsby

This Is Me

T he smallest in class.
H ave times when I'm moody.
I 'm as cheeky as a monkey.
S illy like my sister.

I will always love my family.
S ometimes I get told to do a handstand.

M ostly I wake up tired.
E lephants like amazing, fantastic Dumbo are one of my favourite things to draw, and another could be a delicious Dumbo cake.

Cleo (7)
Western Primary School, Grimsby

This Is Me!

T iny as a baby tortoise.
H appy as a bird flying to Heaven.
I nterested in princess books.
S easide is my favourite place to be.

I really love my family.
S ometimes I play with my sister and her dollhouse.

M e and my sister play hide-and-seek.
E els are my favourite animals because my dream is to be a marine biologist.

Isabella Gladding (7)
Western Primary School, Grimsby

This Is Me

As bright as the night
As dark as the daylight
As pretty as a bee
As ugly as a flower
As hot as an ice cube
As cold as the sun
As sad as dogs
As happy as books

As light as a feather
As heavy as a truck
As tall as a house

As high as a rat

As quick as a snail
As slow as lightning flashing

As brave as a baby hippo.

Lilly (9)
Western Primary School, Grimsby

This Is Me

As nice as a baby

As bright as the night
As dark as the sun

As clever as a teacher
As clever as a baby

As tall as a rat
As small as an elephant
As slow as a cheetah
As quick as a snail

As cute as a lion
As cute as a puppy

As busy as a snail
As lazy as a bee
As funny as a bad dream
As boring as a ride.

Ava-Marie (8)
Western Primary School, Grimsby

Opposites

As fast as a sloth
As slow as an ostrich
As tough as an ant
As weak as a rhino
As wet as a camel
As short as a shark
As boiling as a polar bear
As freezing as a panda
As quick as a sloth
As slow as a cheetah
As lazy as a tiger

As wide as a bear
As kind as a tiger

As nasty as a bunny
As small as the Eiffel Tower.

Lucas Cocks (8)
Western Primary School, Grimsby

As... A...

As cold as a light bulb
As hot as the night
As scary as a balloon
As funny as a spider
As fast as a snail
As slow as a tiger

As smart as a book
As silly as a clown

As happy as a person on the floor
As sad as a ride
As tall as a snail
As short as a giraffe
As kind as a bully
As mean as a dancing butterfly.

Dynasty (8)
Western Primary School, Grimsby

All About You

As bright as a night
As scared as the bright

As loud as a mouse
As loud as an instrument
As sneaky as a ninja
As bald as a random bald man
As sad as losing a dog
As happy as getting a dog
As sharp as teeth
As blunt as a pencil
As thick as a tree
As skinny as a finger.

It's not true, can you take a joke?

Oakley Wiseman (8)
Western Primary School, Grimsby

This Is Me

T rains, I like to see them go by.
H oliday because it will be relaxing.
I celand because it's freezing.
S ongs because I like to sing them.

I mmingham because it's amazing.
S ummer is my favourite.

M aths because I'm amazing at it.
E xciting when someone plays with me.

Lukas Sterry (9)
Western Primary School, Grimsby

This Is Me!

T ea is my favourite drink.
H andsomer than Tom Holland.
I love playing on my Xbox and watching Spider-Man.
S ometimes I am a cheeky monkey.

I would like to be a Spider-Man actor.
S ummer is the best season.

M y future is amazing. I love it now!
E els are electric and I am too.

Joshua Richardson (7)
Western Primary School, Grimsby

This Is Me

As cool as the sun
As warm as ice
As mean as mice
As nice as an angry bull
As tall as a ball
As small as a door

As fresh as mud
As dirty as a frog

As fast as a lake
As slow as a cheetah
As pretty as a donkey
As ugly as a horse
As busy as a statue
As lazy as a bee
As happy as a lonely girl.

Georgie-Rae Wraith (9)
Western Primary School, Grimsby

This Is Me!

As fast as a snail
As short as a whale

As royal as a queen
As buzzed as a bee

As cold as fire
As hot as ice
As quiet as a monkey
As loud as a mouse
As lazy as a bee
As slow as the sea

As pretty as a tree
As ugly as a bee

As straight as a line
As old as time.

Layla Alassaf (9)
Western Primary School, Grimsby

This Is Me!

T his is me!
H amsters and giraffes are my favourite animals.
I love my funny family.
S ing is my favourite movie.

I love to play Roblox.
S inging is my favourite hobby.

M y hair is as smooth and as brown as chocolate.
E veryone is my best friend.

Darby (9)
Western Primary School, Grimsby

Rio The Rapper

This is me,
This is my favourite thing to do,
Playing games,
Like being lame,
Always being the same.
I'm being a pain,
Checking my username,
On YouTube every day,
Yay, yay!
Here today, playing my game.
Eating away,
Shouting, "Yay!"
Playing today like every day!

Rio Harvey (9)
Western Primary School, Grimsby

This Is Me!

As quick as a snail
As big as a nail
As high as your hand

As dry as the sand

As hot as ice
As great as being nice

As dark as the sun

As small as a bun
As fun as a fairy-tale ride
As funny as a slide
As fast as you can tell
As done as you can smell!

Desire (8)
Western Primary School, Grimsby

This Is Me

I am as silly as a monkey.
I am as smart as a teacher.
I am as fast as a cheetah.
I am a super striker.
I am strong and brave.
My eyes are melted chocolate.
My favourite game is Fortnite.
After my favourite thing is eating and sleeping.
This is me!
My nana also calls me a pain.

Oscar (9)
Western Primary School, Grimsby

As, As, As, As

As soft as cat's fur
As rough as a brick
As tall as a tree
As small as a flower
As kind as an angel
As evil as a devil

As happy as a thunderstorm
As sad as a sunny day
As bright as the night

As bright as the sun
As quiet as a fox
As loud as a lion.

Alissia Bartlett (9)
Western Primary School, Grimsby

This Is Me

As bright as a grave
As hungry as a wave
As twisted as a ruler
As warm as a cooler
As ugly as a flower
As quiet as a plougher

As excited as a dog
As tired as a log

As tall as a germ
As stuck up as a worm
As unwise as an owl
As sensitive as a growl.

Michal Palka (9)
Western Primary School, Grimsby

Me, The Poetry!

I am a...

I am a brilliant football striker.
I am a good Roblox player.
I love my cats, Freddy's my favourite.
I am a cheetah, strong and fast.
I am as kind as a helping mum.
My hair is a custard cream biscuit.
My eyes are blue like blueberries.
This is me!

Ben Hammond (8)
Western Primary School, Grimsby

This Is Me!

H appy.
O range juice.
L emonade.
L ambs, baby ones.
I love my family.
E xcellent.

W inter season.
A nimals.
T urtles.
S quiggles, my horse.
O range, the colour.
N oodles.

Hollie Watson (9)
Western Primary School, Grimsby

This Is Me!

I am as strong as a hammer.
My eyes are as grey as a thunderstorm.

As fast as a golden cheetah, I
Run on the field.

My hair is as brown as hot
Chocolate and coffee.

I eat curly pasta that looks
Like a rattlesnake.

This is me!

Ethan Sharp (8)
Western Primary School, Grimsby

This Is Me!

I am as fast as a cheetah.
I like to play with my friends on Fortnite.
I like to eat bananas just like a monkey.
I also like to eat chocolate mint.
I am helpful and caring, I play with my little brother.
I have blue eyes like the deep blue sea.
This is me.

Alfie Rice (8)
Western Primary School, Grimsby

This Is Me

As dark as the sun
As calm as a lion
As loud as a mouse
As ugly as a bride
As hot as ice
As boring as a theme park
As lazy as a bee
As slow as a cheetah
As mean as a newborn puppy
As sad as a dancing butterfly
As tall as a mouse.

Harper Mason (9)
Western Primary School, Grimsby

This Is Me!

I am as sweet as candyfloss
My hair is as long
And as blonde as Rapunzel
I am as shy as a mouse
My eyes are as blue as the summer
Sky
I am as kind as my friends
My smile is as big as the
Cheshire Cat's.
This is me!

Lacie-Jai (8)

Western Primary School, Grimsby

This Is Me!

As tall as a spider
As ugly as a flower
As heavy as a feather
As quiet as a wolf
As cold as a light bulb
As funny as a bad dream
As fast as a turtle
As lazy as a bee
As dark as the sun
As finished as I can be.

Annabeth Cameron (9)
Western Primary School, Grimsby

This Is Me

A kennings poem

I am a...
Piano player,
Song singer,
Picture drawer,
Big sleeper,
YouTube watcher,
Roblox builder,
Dog lover,
Book reader,
And finally...
A big ray of sunshine.

Lilah (7)
Western Primary School, Grimsby

This Is Me!

A kennings poem

I am a...
Minecraft builder
YouTube watcher
Fortnite player
G FUEL drinker
Basketball thrower
Pepperoni pizza eater
A meme appreciator
And finally...
A TikToker!

Kayden (8)
Western Primary School, Grimsby

This Is Me

I am a
Joker
Pink girl
Holiday person
A snowgirl in winter
Pizza girl
And finally...
A happy girl.

Millie Andrews (8)
Western Primary School, Grimsby

YOUNG WRITERS INFORMATION

We hope you have enjoyed reading this book – and that you will continue to in the coming years.

If you're the parent or family member of an enthusiastic poet or story writer, do visit our website **www.youngwriters.co.uk/subscribe** and sign up to receive news, competitions, writing challenges and tips, activities and much, much more! There's lots to keep budding writers motivated!

If you would like to order further copies of this book, or any of our other titles, then please give us a call or order via your online account.

Young Writers
Remus House
Coltsfoot Drive
Peterborough
PE2 9BF
(01733) 890066
info@youngwriters.co.uk

Join in the conversation!
Tips, news, giveaways and much more!

YoungWritersUK YoungWritersCW youngwriterscw